GARDENS OF THE
INTERREGNUM

GARDENS OF THE
INTERREGNUM

NORM SIBUM

BIBLIOASIS
WINDSOR, ONTARIO

FIRST EDITION

Library and Archives Canada Cataloguing in Publication

Gardens of the interregnum / Norm Sibum.
    Sibum, Norm, 1947– author.

Poems.

Canadiana (print) 20200166468 | Canadiana (ebook) 20200166476
ISBN 9781771963398 (softcover) | ISBN 9781771963404 (ebook)

LCC PS8587.I228 G37 2020 | DDC C811/.54—dc23

Edited by Amanda Jernigan
Copy-edited by Emily Donaldson
Typeset by Gordon Robertson

 **Canada Council
for the Arts**   **Conseil des Arts
du Canada**   ONTARIO | ONTARIO
CREATES | CRÉATIF

Published with the generous assistance of the Canada Council for the Arts, which last year invested $153 million to bring the arts to Canadians throughout the country, and the financial support of the Government of Canada. Biblioasis also acknowledges the support of the Ontario Arts Council (OAC), an agency of the Government of Ontario, which last year funded 1,709 individual artists and 1,078 organizations in 204 communities across Ontario, for a total of $52.1 million, and the contribution of the Government of Ontario through the Ontario Book Publishing Tax Credit and Ontario Creates.

PRINTED AND BOUND IN CANADA

— for Marius and Eric

CONTENTS

ASSASSIN BIRD

A warbling creature stated
Its fine reasons to the world.
And I was presented with
All I could want to know.
Oh, this bird was full of itself,
Its handsome throat a musician's pipe.
Here was one of nature's troubadours.

For its wings in flight were songs,
Life and death spelled out,
Chance or predetermination,
God or not, —and as the bird sang, I heard
Apologies for our souls, hard heart rationales
Excusing all the cruelties.

Anywhere I stood, I was always in
Receipt of the song that was the bird.
Venice, Italy? Saskatoon? That endlessly rolling earth
And its heat, tornadoes the weather, the special this:
Hamburger steak, the obligatory peas,
The bent-backed farmers at their plates,
Burned out in that friendly, roadside café,
Remote to the wives, the restive kids—

But the sky's immensity was customary,
The bird the message of the place
Just as it is with birds in every realm,
Love a tease, a roll of the dice
As was the barley crop and the lentil,
Whatever the seed plugged into that prairie.

Time humming in the wind and the wire and
Time in a creaking door and then,

The bird trills some more, the bird lets loose,
Its song a song time out of mind, and now
The last breath that one, in good faith, breathes,
And it's done.

COMMENCEMENT

Bad coffee and God by St Louis Square
Where the old poets went mad, were hipsters, kind of,
So far from the coast, time here more aged,
And I look to begin again.

I've been told, been put to the wise: holy rhymesters
Eluded amateurs, giving the gendarmes the slip.
Verses shinnied up those lovely, squirrel-haunted trees,
Hallucinatory agents on the loose in the blood—

1

Oh, we may as well start here as anywhere else,
Wind on the prowl, dust on the swirl—St Denis,
Rameau in the speakers of the green poutine
Eatery, then Chopin, I think, Polack waltz,
High-heeled girls on errands of mercy
Flitting past. They're almost ghostly, and we've barely commenced.

We've only just gotten this show on the road,
And already questions present themselves:
What about the bad-ass boys, the boys who could care less
If the rules are rigged (the rules are rigged),
Who are what they are in a world that grinds them
Into gemstones of crime or just plain pulp?

What of the boys rolling pitch on the roofs,
The boys in hard hats neck-deep in sewers,
Boys drilling concrete with jackhammers, oblivious
To all the calls for social justice?
Honour precludes them from taking on board

The point of a quarrel, or that they're clueless,
As when Adam addresses Eve, entreats
A dedicated girl with a dedicated treatise:

"It's as clear as the melancholy of a cloudy day:
You're as violet-eyed as ever, you minx,
You small-town creature become complex.
You flaunt your charms for a consideration,
Sell out for a sinecure and call the business
Equal claim to equal compensation."   Now Eve entreats:

"Says you, Mr God's-Gift-To-Women. But wouldn't you know it?
I've charms to flaunt, high charms, low charms, middling charms,
Or so they've been telling me since I graced a crib.
I've got whole worlds in my oyster, whereas you,
Do you think you'll find your precious grail
In that snooker hall to the east of here?"

2

Well, what's in a voice? All of heaven and all of hell
In on the kill, wind on the prowl, dust on the swirl—St Denis,
Geese flying across the skyway, leaves soon to drop—
Power was power before there were laws
To come at the thing as a matter of science,
Wielding a weapon—the primordial rib,
Then polishing an apple—the proverbial one.

Power's power for its own sake and more,
For pity's sake and the sake of living right,
For bragging rights to the store.

Power and other irritants at the heart of life
(Those frisky, frictional forces at play

4

With respect to the severed, sea-going head of Orpheus
Around which prime energies cohere, or not),
Give rise to a jewel. Civilization we call it, *civis*,
Politismós or *Wénmíng*
                              Or the Union Pacific Railway,
The pearl in its cup, its somber sheen
Love's countenance ...
                              One of its mug shots, at any rate—

3

— *I am developing a seminar course called 'A Sociology of Extinction':
Regards, E.C.—*

Power attracts its fêtes, wants its summer getaway spots.
It flies to UNESCO heritage sites.
This city-state so grim in March,
Unearthly in the autumn heat of twilight
(What with the deep maple shadow of back lanes,
The dreamy-eyed Li Po's on the Main), —

This *Sin City,* this *City of Saints,* home to numberless slurs
As when there's no sceptered isle anywhere near
Save for that menace to the south of here,
Is all Lamborghini at a traffic signal,
The revs ear-splitting, trophy girls playing it cool, —
And the sports in the drivers' seats have
Restless macho in their steering hands.
So then, a lull, —
Loner skulks by, looking for hash or a friend.
Somewhere Stephen Hawking, physics man,
Sclerotic, seeking God's mind,
Crumpled in his wheelchair, spins
Down the runway of a fashion show and off the deep end,

And in the hunt for lost gravity he takes along
An army of thieves, assassins, languorous pole dancers—
Red light, green light, you ready to roll?
Tell me when you're ready to go.

4

Who's done mayhem and who's been done?
It's in the wrist, this doing and being done, —
It's in the pout of the male or female or androgyne
Or some other new-world-order paragon,
The vocabularies of finesse and victimhood
As precise as any atomic timepiece.
So much knowledge hard on the knees
As one ascends the steps to the Oratory on one's knees
In this *City of a Hundred Steeples*—

That item of empowerment, eyes on the margins?
Someone must marry the builder of stadiums.
Someone will be privy to the mysteries of the fix.
Converse with her, you'll swear she's a fixer,
Her mandate men, culture, and pharmaceuticals.
Listen again, you'll know beyond doubt
The strategies are as ageless as the hills.
Earth-like planets in far-off conglomerates?
There's corn to harvest, blood to extract
From mephitic rocks in cold, cold space.
                (In the meantime, McGrath the poet —
Off the cuff God man, out of synch with prayer —
He wants a rhyme, no more than that, no less
As he takes his lunch on the lunchtime *terrasse*.)

Irish from the get-go, born by the sea
Two thousand miles this side of a spit of land
Christened Dingle, given to lounge wear, firing off
Singularities in both official tongues, Italian too, stuffed to the gills
With Buddhist principles, the village cinema
And Gable and Cooper flickering on the screen, —
Fastest rhymester west of Rimouski
And in the vulgate, even so our poet is
A poster boy for what portends.

And what's portended, it goes by
On tire tread, on car, bus, truck, and perambulator tread, —
Swooshes by on the tread of bicycles,
Saunters past on the crepe soles of agitprop,
On those cloven hoofs there,
While the alphabet soup in the onion bowl spells
The swansong of a poet, the martini semi-arid.
This befits a desert rat of a maritime province.
And as the poet awaits the imminent rhyme,
For some sergeant-at-arms to thump the floor
With authority's mace at the least hint of one,
His childhood, and it was kind of sacred—his pubescent years,
Recalls nothing so much as a few set-pieces:
The wormy cod, the picturesque
Or the local deadbeat on the slatternly porch,
The worm-eaten dory on the beach.
McGrath thinks to renew his vow:
To literature he'll consign his heart and mind,
His come-easy, his go-easy genius shade.
But will literature have his carcass?
"The flesh is sad, alas. May I trouble you for the sauce?"

And Zsa Zsa the waitress, less from Budapest
The more she hails from Rivière du Loup
And fans herself with the bill of fare,
Might say to him while we exchange
Our parting shots, our fare-thee-wells:
"Monsieur, here's mud in your eye.
Oo-la-la. Sweet life. *Ça donne un méchant buzz—*"

Oh, she'd spark the poet, had she a mind to.
There it is—what drives a poet to drink:
Not want of rhyme but the lack
Of divinity that would take
The edge off loneliness,
Verse no substitute,
Verse a trifle,
Verse a hoot.

Incomplete, as ever, we remain chock-full
Of unease, the days and nights unsecured.
We're the image, even now, of gods we trashed.
We're the guttering ache in our hearts.
We're those walking sores we see every day
Here, there, and everywhere, and keep
At arm's length.

ANACREON REDUX

Though I drink my drink and thrum my guitar
And receive kisses due me on the cheek
As if I were a potentate, —

Though I tickle the muse and stick out my tongue
When it snows, the stars in their numbers newly increased
Three-fold, —though I read thick books and admire the girls
And visit sick persons in hospital wards

Some of whom have brave love-curls,
And I bring them newspapers and contraband, —

Though I commit rhyme against pretense
Be it state-sanctioned, be it off-the-wall,
Be they rhymes at which I used to look askance,
Rhymes for all manner of ad hoc committees or congresses,
It seems I'm only a poet, after all, no cape-wearing oracle,
Drifting from island to island, polis to polis,

Debacle to debacle, heartbreak to heartbreak,
The lyrics in my bones sparkling in a diamond-edged sun.

THE MORNING AFTER HARRY BUMGARNER'S NIGHT OF POKER

— Wherewithal shall a young man cleanse his way?

1

Harry, my man, in your person you haul
New subject matter from pillar to post.
Consumer of zinc, Omega-3 fats,
You're a pumpkin-seed chewer, a size 12 in shoes, athlete of
What has cachet in new virtue, your toes angled
To the left of the rightward-slinking centre.

Otherwise, in your two-and-a-half rooms you keep
Your powder dry, there by the funeral home,
The coin store, the diner where
You can still get smoked meat as good
As the divine meat your fathers ate,
You purist when it comes to meth rock,
In beer strictly blonde—

Lover-boy loner the girls go for,
Though they hate it that you still cause them to want
To tickle your chin, you're god haunted. Who saw that coming?
Among your friends, you laugh it off, —
You shrug away your notions of cause
Lest all the op-eds and the science
Show you up as a complete dufus
And write you off as an utter ass.
Bottom dollar, you're a romantic,
A refuge for complexities that no shrink

Would think to waste good pixie dust on and yet,
In this our neo-lib order, we are in everything
Permitted, allotted, allowed and bought.

2

Memorizer of verse, you're a poet's last hope.
Stalker after fictions, you're a novelist's wet dream,
His reason to pursue his futility.
World-wide traveller, Canada your carry-on, you browse through
The philosophers at cruising altitude.
But Monsieur Sartre? Are you sure? Would he be
Your stitch in time such as saves nine
Extinction events from coming to pass?
Moreover, on the morning after the poker game went down,
(It was your little domestic touch) a rose in its vase still stood tall
There on the card table. No collective's banter, no nicotine cloud
Managed to wilt it. *Lord, have mercy upon us and incline our hearts*
To keep this law—

Dusky symbol of wisdom and love,
Of what's holy in the blood, this infinitely foliate valentine,
Single bloom in a clear vase of clear water, —
The flower fresh in the cool morning light,
And it remained oracular even as
The heat began stinking up the place, —
This rose-comedian genuflected
To a pair of sixes, good enough for the bluff and driving from the field
So-and-So's politics and his aces, —this rose-comic with its air
Of knowing what all your secrets are
Gave its nod to time and space, and to the resurrection, too,
That, like a tent city, sprang up in your eyes
When last you attended mass, *and make thy chosen people joyful—*

Half-empty bag of crisps athwart it
(As were the filthy ashtray, the dead soldiers, the bottle of wine
Drained of *in vino veritas*, and then, the greasy cards
Scattered about)—it spoke well of your passions putting in downtime,
So much so a fellow believed
The odds would tilt his way
And his for now unvisited bed
Would host a better faith.

3

And the leaves are turning, or by next week
They will have metamorphosed, with colour decked out,
So many party dancers at a hoedown
Of deep-souled penitents mad
For quantum perusals of love and infinite life.
The noble army of martyrs praise thee.

And just as the libertarian, maintaining reason, sacrifices sense, —
Just as the attentive psychopath only meant
To cull the public's cradle of corrupt inhabitants, —
Just as the good doctor's miracle drug
Is what the system needs (but damn if you can have the use of it),
You want love's physic now, if not yesterday.

So did I, useless for that to which I was born,
The next bubble of promise always a lock,
The next election cycle the next bullseye,
The next sham poem the next Great Gala,
The next Great Love the next sleaze-divorce,
And then, one gets a little snaky—

I should shove over, shouldn't I, and give
The next young guy his shot at failure,

Ever so tricky the choosing which
Investment opportunity to ride
All the way to some patch of glowing sand,
To drinks and lunch, compliments of the house
At Armageddon's Caesar's Palace.
Once a warrior of the word, now I heckle.
Been at it for a thousand years,
All quarrelsome one century, all lovey-dovey
In the next, beauty never a thing to snub,
Truth a casualty of who we are—

4

To more humdrum matters in which I play a humble part—

Here's how it was: one rummaged,
Roaming through ghostly shops of ghostly books.
Still looking for that Ennius to no avail.
You'd think you could find him parked
Between the romances and the local horrors.
You'd think he'd have a goodly spot
Between the DVDs and the histories of art—
Settle down, Harry, I'm getting to you—
Foreign agent? Sleeper cell of one?
I was a stay-at-homer, a misanthrope's misanthrope
Parked at my kitchen table, sleeves rolled up,
Dealing out hands of solitaire,
Hearing out the traffic reports.
The rubbies, the junkies, and all
The comrades of chagrin, they knew, before I did,
That the writing was on the wall
Of a west coast socialist hall.
Beliefs die. Old evils give way

To fresh kills. *We believe that thou shalt come*
To be our judge.

Here's what you've got to look forward to, Harry:
Memorabilia. Dust. Mementos. More dust.
That photograph of Gibbs. Kodak Gold Plus.
Her bosom was aromatic, a richly pungent nosegay of
Gardenia-scented isotopes, that day when, with a rotten egg, she
    thought

                        To bring an executive closure
                        And only winged the podium—

5

Here's what else is coming for you
Both now and in revolution's after-life:
Pindaric echoes of unabashed snobbery
And all the fine print of unintended consequence.
So you ran the marathon in the year
That saw you a legal ballot-stuffer
And you didn't lose your breakfast
Or win the battle or lose the war,
Though another girl presented you with your pink slip.
She was good for any barricade and any Eros,
She who pointed a finger: you still a child.
Did you criminally lick her ear?
Was it the gelato at Enrico's, the magic realism
That showed you up as an amateur lacking gravitas?
The sea is his, and he made it, —and his hands
                  Prepared the dry land—

As I pick through my brain for what went wrong,
For how I was meant to live
According to the dictates of faith and reason,

And sport and art and other decadence, —
As I keep myself company with artifacts—
Antique Parker pen, tattered Tacitus, —
As I recall Nixon's grand paranoia
And Jimmy Carter's smile, the "Hi ya"
That was lost on Iran and the GOP,

You might laugh, and you may as well laugh out loud,
But I fear the departmental voice that leers
The joke's on you. Or else there's a richer trove of purpose
On the moon's dark side where the strings get pulled.
Or else that dark side is a situation room
Where one makes nice or makes nasty.
Special ops: one gets it on with street urchins
Playing all ends against the Top Dog,
And there's Clinton in her groove—

6

Now Harry, old boy, you're not one of those, are you, who believe
The hype that your life's a junket,
Your ticket punched, your bags X-rayed,
From Here to Eternity stitched on your brow?
You think it's at par, the guff your broker peddles?
That you'll hit the ground running, trumping reality as you go,
When you alight again on a speck of earth,
Soon to give the natives plenty to do? Are you the enemy of my
      enemy?
Winter, and you up against it, it could be you'll be shovelling my
      driveway
For a bit of cash. It could be you're a man who could write
                              Berlin Alexanderplatz
But will write instead
                  A plethora of *Tartuffes.*

To sum up, I've been inert a while, lying low,
Low magnetic readings parlaying sparks
Into high obscurities of verse. I've had tropes to spare
As well as deep background truths
                                        For Aphrodite, Psyche, Bacchus too,
Languid in the Byzantine twilight.
I regret nothing—I rue it all—
The affections sworn by, divorces incurred.
The vegetative gods and Tammuz and his retinue
Were a kind of dictation, a fait accompli
In the coursing of our blood
As we dreaded moody April,
The Easter time of year.
O Lord, open thou our lips.
"Alright, someone deal. Harry, what's with this damn bloom of yours?"
"Crisps? Is this all there is to eat?"
"What? We drank all the beer?"

One dreads the Easter time of year, the awful contemplation of
Chocolate bars and trumpet blasts,
Agrigento, hill town of countless epochs,
And I was semi-archaeological, Orpheus swinging by
To bugger Priscilla in the shower,
Her Cupid's-bow mouth rebuking
The suburban values that mightily bored her,
A symphony of bells in the bell towers
Chatting up God, charming the Austrians,
And one's attendant dreams of justice. So you won't bear with me then,
You under-educated, over-pedigreed, under-paid successor
To the humanist creed, you, after all, so much more than I

The subject of this poem, the subject of
A million forces, a million pressures
And the squeeze play put upon you
The day you were born: how pay the rent
Without trifling with your character.
I may without hypocrisy
Affirm the truth, detract no man,
But do all things with equity—
Well, I understand. You must go your way
Or you won't have a way at all.
And even then, no guarantee.

WHAT GOES AMISS

The Sunday picnics after church,
Hotdogs, colas, the cream pies,
The homemade relish, the lemonade
In tall, cold pitchers cold to the hands
All are lodged in memory, that seasonal traveller always wanting
Its old room back. Men assembled on the sun-swept grass
Shagging down slow-arcing drives—
Untroubled grace—

I

       Hatless Mr Niedermann, he's just run
A fly ball down, inning over. He trots in
From the playing field, well-oiled glove
Tucked under his arm. A comfortable chinking of keys and coins
In the pocket of his Sunday slacks . . .
Who plays in their Sunday best?
He sprawls now alongside his wife,
Her eyes bright with something—but with what?—
She at rest in the shade of the elm
Like a figure in a Manet.

Hatless Mr Niedermann who was proof of love,
He tips back a gold can of beer that's been on ice.
He has a loving look for his slim and gracious,
Inward-looking, childless love, and in her smile both here and far away,
There's a glimmer of her faith in him.
And all around them husbands and wives
Pass infant prodigies back and forth
So that mothers might smoke
Or fathers lope back to the field,

Everything familiar, everything burdensome, —
And the infectious grins are everyday.

Infectious grins are what I recall,
As if, once, the people had good reason to be thankful.
What a grin the girl with the coiled pigtails had,
Her socks so white they hurt one's thoughts—

But into the young body of Mrs Niedermann something crept,
Or else it originated there—treacherous, —
Something not a toy-like credo, something not a play-doll chapel
Not the Almighty Dollar, not Sears-Roebuck,
Not Curtis LeMay— "kill all them Japs,"
Not liberty, —something sinister perhaps
Out of nature, perhaps a disease of mind.
And she with her kind ways, with her wavy black hair,
The pleasing smile-lines that led from her eyes
To a place that just might've been my soul, —
She whom I liked more than I liked my mother, —
She who read a thousand books and pondered much,
So much so, her man got used to it, —
She in whom I caught just a hint
Of a woman living under strain
But who couldn't name the strain, no more than I could,

Was consumed, was digested by a sickness,
And I could see only the dying smile
And the bed of sickness, —
Dashing husband now a wreck,
Isolate in his empty God-belief,
Love no wall that keeps out un-grace,
Some angel-less swoon in the gut the living farce.
There's always death to take the place
Of what goes amiss—

II

Gone, too, the cowboy shirt with its pearl snaps.
A boy wore it in and out of doors.
The shell six-shooter, holster and caps,
The solitary suns of all the lonely afternoons—
They belong to another day. They're dead, they're dying, they sing
Hymns no more, are innocent no longer, never were—
Parishioners of a Missouri valley he knew.
The god was as much tick fever as He was
Catfish and slaw, and the God of the Book, —
As was Crane Creek, Civil War skirmish there,
And the Unionists guarding the telegraph wires—

III

On the sandy beach of a cold, green lake
Not yet famous for its rave parties,
His mother at work on her movie tan,
Woman's Own in her polished hands,
Mrs Niedermann about to pass away
To somewhere dark and beyond retrieving,
Betrayal puts a boy out of kilter,
His mother in no mood for his sulk:
Look, she isn't long for this world.
Stop your whining. Run along, play.
No one and nothing lives forever.
The soft drinks stand in his sight,
With its bright pennants and 'Drink Nehi' sign,
Colas, candy bars, American flags, begins to dislodge
Bijou crucifixion scenes and
A sickbed from his pious mind.
"They have their lives and we have ours," she says
Of farmers and their spouses and their prayers.

"Your father has his, by the way, the skunk.
Aren't you ready for your first kiss?
Ready for a girl who doesn't wear braces?
You could take her for a boat ride on the lake.
Look at those slackers from the faith—"

IV

Eighty-nine years, and she's departed the life,
The green storm skies her Missouri phase,
She in terror, always, of Allied bombs
Especially on nights of lightning and thunder.
Berlin girl, and it never occurred to her,
She with dreams of romance and a life of purpose,
To refuse the idolatry of power,
Though of the war on terror she said:
"Déjà vu."

V

And she'd be the first to tell you all you wished to know
About the Russians and the camps they ran.
She'd hand him talking points
Long-distance on the telephone,
And she'd win back the love
A son ought to have for his mother.
But the republic that they were asked to cherish
With its boasts, its aims, its whispers and crimes,
Got to be careworn, as always happens,
One foot already in a shade that charms.

OCTOBER POEM

— to AP

You accorded to the page the words that follow:
    'Winter days of silver and palest gold.'
    In so doing, you flirted with danger,
    But made out like a bandit at large.
Yellow leaves in this October blow just now
    Are all a-sail and tinged with red.
    It's as if, from above and overnight,
    A mist of blood was loosed
    In the course of a sacrificial rite.
Now that I've said as much, will the earth crack open,
    Swallow me up, and then close over
    A moving violation on the run?
    Will you accord to your page an observation?
    "Dear lad, that one, but his narrative sprawls."
    No one expects a god, these days, to snap his fingers
    And briskly rouse one from the cold, cold grave.
    Then again, look at what's gone missing
    In the deal that brought us our emancipating charter:
    Shame for the shabbiness, clear-eyed contrition,
    Box seats for Rossini's *Stabat Mater,*
    Sung by the angels, Muti at the helm.

o

Caligula may've been a vicious monster,
Or else he was stuck with a bad press.
Built a bridge to span the Bay of Naples.
Have you ever seen the glitter of the sea in the Bay of Naples?
    (So, you've seen the splendid fireworks,
    And you're a better woman for it.)
Caesar, flaunting genius, drove

A gleaming chariot with dual pipes
    Over the signal achievement of his engineering feat.
Crowed he was great, as great as that guy
    Alexander the Macedonian.
Cowed Poseidon the moody god
Into shushing his ill-tempered waves:
    God with trident smoothed
The waters for a Roman stunt.
Lies old and new are one and the same,
    Humankind god-like with its works,
    Divinely sparked, divinely loosed.
    Such a bother, our hearts couched
    In theological packages . . .

    o

What with the glitter of the sea,
Naples woke up the amorous mystic in me.
Anarchist with nerves of steel,
I took on board your words,
    Your 'winter days of silver and palest gold,'
    And with this necklace of bravura
    I lassoed fat necks and called it justice,
Your sentiment put to lovely use.
Naples, however, caused you to favour
    The diplomat's pouch: "Outrage is outré, and we each have
    Our talents, our little fund of savoir faire,
Genius lodged in every
Butcher, baker, candlestick maker."
All parade-ground bark, I begged to differ:
    "Genius? Oh yes. In every mind a flame.
    The gods once owned the copyright for the flame.
    Bureaucrats, critics, and art's networks
    Have long since copped the song."

    o

And now old because young no longer,
To be young again is a ruse hard to master.
Out of misplaced sympathy, friends play along
And call you a phenomenon.
    You see how it is: my shoddy display of aplomb
    In respect to life's conundrums—
But as for loving like once we loved
In the way the music of our youth would've had us love—with all our
    hearts
    And not too much of our heads, it's in the picture, this sleight-of-
    hand,
    The ruse-maker's ardor as wide as the sun,
    As easily spooked as a soul out of his depth.
    For love and the objects of love's desire
    Are ephemeral, always moving
    In the mirror of the sea's constant motion, —
Are as still as snow will soon be when
    It falls and comes to lie quietly
    In the white birch woods of Quebec, the wind died down.

STARLING NATION

Ask why those glossy, iridescent birds
Of a sudden will shroud a tree,
And in their mimicry sound off
Like man-made machines?
Hear back: safety in numbers.
Hear back: scale-free correlations—mathematics to you—explain
The seemingly choreographed, evasive flight patterns.

o

And there I was on the back porch
In the course of a predictably human day
Under a cold, blue sky, under the thumb
Of satellite signals and other buzz,
All the engineers of the popular will.
There I was with my votive thoughts
As hot water warmed the whisky
And a cheroot added to the ceremony,
Scarf around my throat, wonder around my brain.

Such a ruckus in the maples,
Such bone-rattling chorusing
Those starling chortlers were making
In the hollows of my ears:
A scene out of Wagner, out of something mad,
A world before humankind, Jurassic parliament,
The sun the earliest god.

And then in an instant they were gone, —
They'd advanced in their swarms, in their murmurations
To other objectives, other trees, other neighbourhoods.
A pair of jays inherited the silence
While a crow lumbered from branch to branch,

The instigator perhaps, heckler shouted down.
And I was no wiser than before, but I was humbled:
What fear in those creatures, what deep-ranging response
To all that would undo their starling nation.

A TIP OF THE CAP TO SUETONIUS

The split-screen affair of White House scandal,
As timeless an enterprise as the spring season
And the promise of fruit-heavy trees to come
In Charlevoix or Montérégie, had me in its thrall,
The many voices of a pundit panel
Merging into a lonesome canary chirp,
The innuendo in the clamour
As ripe as anything in Suetonious.
Even so, where was the scandalous sex? Where the omens,
The anomalies in nature, deformed bodies
On the wrong side of the gods or a drug bust?
Ah, better late than never—here they are:
The comic's squib, reportage and satire: that bit
About the golden showers. And the pasquinades that reverence
The small, near porcelain hands.

INTIMACIES

I

The wind rolled through the maples as if to say,
"Here's where I live, here in this place."
It set upon the cherry tree in Mrs Orlow's yard,
The old woman gone from her rooms, ground floor.
She, poor dear, was packed off, sent
To a facility where, her wits confounded,
She'll die perplexed, the world not the world
Into which she was born, the nursing staff's palaver
                            alien to her mother-tongue.
Black cloud above, edges moon-lit,
Was moving fast, with all the spirit
Of lovers seeking rendezvous, of assemblies of soldiers presenting
    themselves.
Fructifying rain, perpetual showers,
And everything's extra-lush this year
With deep shadows: fern, vine, shrub, the wind itself.
                    The blooms are fat.
Nietzsche was more of a friend to God
Than he was to those who swore by their pews.
My neighbours swear by *Mon pays*,
By tam-tams and trip advisories.
New physics might have more to say for things
Than science that's had it all its way when it comes
To sleep disorders, to peeping Toms,
Neutrinos, cottage spiders,
To the lengthening tenure of autocratic rule.
Then again, Pascal's Principle, and the deluge
    might just seek its own level and drown the who,
    what, where, why, and how of these things.

II

On the balcony, a jury of one,
I was musing, smoking, inhabiting my skin.
The rain, the wind and the dark made
For an hour when a pilgrim could hear
Mothers in the area break into plainchant
Echoing up to cloud-covered stars:
"To bed with you now. Brush your teeth."
I was enjoying the lustre of evening things,
The sweet darkness of the twilight rain,
Nothing nefarious in the wind.
There was alarm, to be sure, but no urgency
In the sirens tearing through the street.
The next building over, it was not the case:
Sex on the brain, Gordon was acting up again.
Impossible not to hear him through his window,
This sandlot Zeus, this glassy-eyed centaur
Whinnying forth a string of moans, —
This slack-jawed, gummy Endymion
Whom the once smitten moon now can't stand, —
This over-the-hill gladiator with tattooed arms.
His bliss weighing heavy on all our souls,
Something in the man was bent on dying.
For Gordon was self-pleasuring or, lucky him, enabled,
Honouring his portion of the priapic dance.
And then, and I couldn't determine the gender
Of the figure in white … at any rate, Victoria or Vic
Stepped into the lane and checked things out,
Leaned up against a vine-clad fence and dropped
          his or her trousers and squatted.

III

You sit out quiet-like. Thoughts, unasked for, flood the mind
As if pumped from a well not your mind,
All that you see thought-generated,
Constructs of memory the moment now:
How a kiss tasted, how an embrace lied.
        Propped against the vine-choked fence,
        Was he or she an emissary in disguise,
            Doing the business in the kindly dark?

I turned my eyes away, the intimacy illicit.
Had the border police a stake in this?
Man or woman or other entity
Might have been a stray,
Might have been in between party raves,
Upstart angel in search of relief.
            The sigh said as much.
When next I looked the interloper,
Maenad, satyr, alleyway flasher,
Blinded by pent-up energies, had moved on.
The sky was clearing, Saturn on course
To maintain its elliptical orbit around the sun.
I took the measure of Schopenhauer:
The beer he drank, the sausages he ate, the hours in which
He thought his thoughts, laughed and wept
And scratched the ears of his poodle Butz.
Took the measure of Nietzsche again,
The abyss, lisp and all, teasing him:
"Little Pastor, I'm at my ease.
You're the sourpuss off your medicines."

IV

And Gordon, having had his pleasure,
Was on his feet, swaying side to side—a mangy bear.
He was bellowing threats into a mobile phone
Against the backdrop of a ducal palace.
Someone owed him, owed him now,
The drift in his booze-heavy voice
Impregnated with new protocols:
Pay up or he'd unleash the pit-bulls.

V

Consolations are illusory and so, merciful.
Every heaven is carved from desire's jade.
Every enclave is subject to the lurid effects
Of naked light bulbs, of commodes malodorous or not,
Of the replays out of season: *he shoots, he scores,* —
Wind on the rise yet again, more cloud cindery black,
Crying children, dads wanting their mindless youth back,
The dog whining in the yard all a-wonder:
Why had his kind bonded with this species?
It prepares the field with innuendo and rape.
Then sanctions apply, and then the warheads,
And who now will wipe the blood from us?

CREATION TALE

You'd think I'd learned, but here I go again
To bother the muse and toss stones at her
Black window, disturbing her sweet, delicious dreams.

And here she is, her spiteful nature
Born of time and its roll-out sweep,
Chilly words rolling off her lips:

"Some world you've gone and engendered, boy.
For this I had to pop open my eyes,
My crypt so cozy, poem-proof?"

Crack of thunder. Flash of light.
For the briefest instant a blinded penitent has his sight:

How it is that poetry and justice once
Came to us in the same utterance.

SNOW CAPITAL

Windless night, and we remarked
On the snow and how it fell
As so many crystalline parachutes
Of an armada in the air.
Smoke break on Marko's porch.
Wise men on a toot.
Beloved Montreal,
Poetry's snow capital ...

Then one among us saw fit to quip, with respect to the Minister,
That he was his mother's son—the PM.
What's more, bananas are high in potassium.
But for Akhmatova and her marking time
With Pushkin in the course of a siege
(St Petersburg, and the chokehold
That was nine hundred days and one million dead
By way of Army Group North's loving clinch),
Things were anything but good. Who in the crushing cold had the
    stamina
For the making of verses in a dream?
Who had the energy for dining on
A crumb, a shoe, or human meat,
Let alone go jitterbugging now
In some starlight cabaret?

o

All equilibriums being states of nature, we
The inheritors of a consciousness
The savannah with its tall grasses helped to shape,
Shunting desert to lush pampas and back again, —

We, by way of verses, by dint of drugs, investigated
The state of our psyches on Marko's porch,

Went and whipped parts of Apollo
And combined them in a mixing bowl
With measures of Dionysus,
The outcome a classic cake the likes of which
        would do for an assassin's teatime snack, —

Would feed ragtag rebels in the Sierra Maestra
Encamped among the owls and parakeets,
Executive dementia in the icing sugar,
The settling of accounts to be carried out
By border patrols on the poor of Peoria—
A snow scene of steeples and snow-caked boughs.
Missing: the chime pearls of sleigh bells . . .
A dream of Pushkin charmed a poet,
The nightmare outside her window
Relenting a little: the ice-hard grins of the dead beyond
Her dream-enclosed mind. Would that our poetry
Had even a sliver of that saving grace. . . .

And the snow falling before our eyes could have been
A poem the sky spoke in a whisper,
Sound crucified with silence.
As if the quiet could trip an alarm.
As if our voices distilled in a crucible of snow
Went on a tear, were quick to punchlines and laughter.
Literary to a fault, steeped in news,
New horrors priming new tableaux,
We vented and reasoned and drew
Verbal vignettes in that air
Of falling snow and demise.
"Hey, man, free will, there's the ticket.
I'm up for that, always am, even if there's none,
                none to save us from ourselves."

And a wise man's wise words hung there
As if subject to a sudden up-gust of wind

Before the resumption of the descent,
It being noted that his thought was superfluous,
Hardly an epitaph for the human condition.
And now, words spent, we were chilled and smoked out,
Neither new men nor old, of no party or cause,
Courageous and cowardly, daunted, undaunted,
Fatalists and addicts, poetry the sacred ampule, —
And we went for the whisky and warmth inside
And the rolling eyes of our better halves.

SIBYLLINE PATCHWORK

Those Romans, they understood—
Try as they might to seal the cracks
Of a dodgy edifice under stress—
The sibylline patchwork cemented over
With oracles dashed off in hexameters—
That the madness was always a stitch shy
Of coming undone, and the big cheat was eternity
    Feeding the empire its sweet nothings.

Tiberius Caesar, that old goat
Who eased his night terrors with self-prescribed
Love nips in the imperial pool,
Was he not the law's chief officer,
Attorney-general to the ceremonies of power
And bleaker nights of the Roman soul?
Did he not take on his scabrous head,
His grim, sour, pustular head,
The inclinations of the rabble
To have bread without labour,
To have labour without unions,
To get rich and get blotto and ride
The endless, the undying
Orgasm all the way to Yuma
And maintain a modicum of order,
    Calling it, what else, *The American Experience*?

If no one has it in for you,
If no satellite, no hidden monitor
Tracks your aura, your heat signature,
The market has you in its grip, —
Marketing lights up your particulars,
Which way you'll lean, which way you'll jump

Should the moon, of a sudden, slip its orbit.
  (This too is as you like it,
    Your most intimate shudder on the books.)

But lover of love, sports enthusiast,
Patriot for hire at minimum wage,
Artist without an ethos to defend,
Stuck for the rest of your glory days
With all the revelry of fat chance, —
Be you rich, poor, loved, abandoned,
Be you Petronius Arbiter or Gloria Vanderbilt,
Believer or a skeptic's why, —
Be you the dreaded minotaur
For whom truth is a consideration
Or what's useful to a lie, —
Whether you party with the Rat Pack
Or shuffle along in chains, no matter:
Your shadow is your stammering oracle
    And that oracle is your vestigial brain

Which advises you don't look back.
Ancient sybils and their cryptic chatter
    Won't right a foundering framework.

It cautions don't look ahead
On account of those cracks in the composition,
Those warps in the massive beams
That bear the weight of the sky
Packed with the souls of collateral damage.
What to do now, your life bristling
As it passes by you, self-involved,
Skittish hound in no mood
To sit or fetch or raise its paw
Or learn new tricks, so ripe are the once loyal eyes
With famine, fear, and the vertigo of
    Broken desire, of belonging nowhere?

DREAM ASSASSIN

There was sleep in which dreams arose
Of literature under glass.
Ancient books opened up
And I read the dead languages
Of God chatter and corn accounts
And the boasts of kings.

There was sleep visited by the laughter
Of old loves come to see me.
And there were sorrows too, and then
The I-told-you-so's went and soured love.
There was sleep which knew no rest,
None of that in the whirling cosmos above,
Birth perpetual in its shadow,
Dying endless, our lot written there,
And space expands to accommodate more.

Truncated, fitful sleep.
Intermittent shuteye.
There was always an insomniac's study
And how many shades of dark a room might carry.

Sleep from which I might emerge, crying out,
Objecting to the program.
It was but egoism on my part.
To think I had a better design . . .

Sleep that novels richly depict—
Sleep that speaks to little fears—
Sleep that fills in phantasms with the light of dawn—
Sleep darkened by the wings of crows—

Sleep that not only brought me her,
But what it was she was born to do.
Sleep that brought no instruction.
Well, what is the mission?

Oh, a blind man taps his forehead.
Agent of change? Assassin? Muse?
She's never the one you think she is.
Lover? Sidekick? Best of friends?
She hardly knows herself (and you oughtn't tell her)
At what or at whom to take aim and yet,
For all her newfound purpose,
She was always dangerous.

3 FOURTEENERS

1

Squirrels plume up and down the trees,
Equal measures grace and farce.
With their eyes they make canticles
To some still-point in a chaos.
The law of pain which is mind and body
Undoes us in the end, sex, death, and abandoned rage
The distillates in every hell, the paternal boughs of tall, wide maples
Overhanging the touchstones of
Crucified laundry in the sun.

It's unstable—the design. So I muttered as I walked
Out beyond the mouldering catacombs
And the roadside bric-a-brac of death.
But that was Rome. Montreal's a border town too,
Realms passing away, realms coming due—

2

Persons more mature than I, silver-haired
In the game of life that is not life,
That's but a compact made of membership,
Have in spades that which crowns their lives,
Indicating tenure: love, sex, money, honour,
All systems go for nailing down power.
And sparrows carve boulevards in the air.

I'm all for pleasure but, even so,
What of the lust that respects no love? The rebels you see
Who know something's off—but what, exactly?

They're butterflies flitting in reverse
So as to inch along again. Our faith in reason—
Such a sick joke, stickpin in the abdomen.
Woke this morning the butt of dreams again.

3

Betrayal at the start brings on the pleasure.
The game gets rougher: you neither win nor lose,
Worn down by the weather in the territories of love.
The hurt of Attis in you, you're as old as all that,
As old as men unmanning themselves
So as to dance in crazed pain for a goddess's smile.
It dazzles as brightly as a winter sun.

You're young still, young enough not to know
That poetry explains nothing, indistinguishable
From time-out-of-mind religions, some Absolute Voice
As worn as stone, as new as rainwater: a festering wound.
Cumulus moves with the sheen of pearls in the blue above
And boys on bikes scoot down the lane
As if love were velocity and the silent birds—

ANGELS OF RECTITUDE

With virtue comes the ordered life.
With virtue comes book-jacket blurbs.
With virtue—but never mind.
I mean to speak of a young woman.
I mean to say, "What can I say? Saw her seemingly miscast,
Customer at a church bazaar:
Heaps of cookies, cakes, and books."

Genial God-assenters milled about
And surly unbelievers scouted for
First editions and curiosities,
Other riffraff of the printed page,
Fingered travelogues and how-to manuals,
Collocations of high discourse.
                              And each fetid daisy of a text
That was a Taylor Caldwell or a D.H. Lawrence
Hemorrhaged form, content, style,
Was pencilled in for a bargain's price.
And time, time was the 'hair of Siva'—
(As featured in *National Geographic*,
October, 1960). And time was a wilted Christ
On a wilted stem
In any year—

o

Nestled between her arm and side
Was romantic trash that I knew
To be set in Bucharest—Fascist era. I might've vented then and there
If only to dismiss the book she held
As well as head off at the pass
Designer fiction and French theory.
But I was dumbstruck. You might say my tongue bombed,

Layabout Adonis out for the count
In a dry vestibule. Moreover,
No labyrinth made of language and terror
Was going to snare and rid the world
Of psychopathic mercenaries,
Let alone incommode a spell.
At best, our orbits run parallel—
Hers, mine, and necessity's—
Every blue moon or so in outlaw space,
The attraction cyclical—

o

So then, as if we were both obliged
To register with some authority
Unconscious intent on each our parts,
And a review board was deliberating,
Our paths crossed without incident:
A narrow squeeze between two bins of glory
Saw us trade places on the floor, and we resumed
Combing through lost states of mind
For their relics. Perhaps she was a poet or a nurse
Shift-weary, bone-tired, overworked.
(Or so I allowed myself to surmise,
Casuist compounding egregious error.)
Would the plot that wormed its way
Through the chapters of the tome that was her purchase
Honour her as-yet-undeclared soul?
Must we all be customs inspectors?

o

I watched her eyes the colour of
A Greek-island sea absorb and reject
The gloating tenor of an argument
As she turned the pages of a book of lectures:
Church Leaders in Primitive Times.

Tertullian jumps the pagan ship, —
Apollo gives way to the Holy Ghost.
Someone's chance mention of Aquinas
Was akin to a reminiscence: "Remember when
Two bits got you a doorman and an usher
In the theatres on Ste Catherine's?"

o

Then a Scotsman with pickled nose,
Adamant with a toothy dialect
And views to the left of Josef Stalin,
Held aloft, as if a severed head, Winston Churchill's
A History of the English-Speaking Peoples. Whereupon the woman
With burgundy scarf and burgundy hair
And the stooped shoulders of disappointment
Eloped with destiny, vacated the scene. Kindly old gent at the exit,
Salt of the earth in a workingman's shirt,
On the look-out for corporate spies and petty thieves,
Bid her adieu, goodbye, and a
Heartfelt adios.

o

                             I would've taken her for a drink, —
She would've gotten fulsome with her rage.
Don't you know? Well, didn't I know
How stinking it was: art galas, the military-industrial complex,
Each and every Palestine, the sex
That's cash-flow in a panderer's pocket, —
The shabby truths, the shabbier lies, the animal cunning
That runs the trains and stocks the stores—
All that
So many shiny baubles of
Ideological fixations, so many hallucinogenic cubes of sugar?
I followed after, chasing—I can't say what—
A clue to the riddle of my existence?

o

                                    Even so, the street, muted showcase of
Well-toned dwellings and lush curtains,
Rich maple shadow, burnished liquors,
High-gloss vehicles, amiable Labradors,
Seemed to have swallowed her.
She'd vanished, as they say, into thin air.
                                    And now
A crowing chorus of angels in my head.
Now a swelling tide of voice.
Now a sweet song to an end of unwanted things.
Now the crunch, the mayhem, the selling-out,
The all-encompassing rectitude
That follows the cessation of hostilities.
Whether or not it was on her part a plan,
She'd had her way with my worst instincts.
She had it in mind to test my mettle.
She had notions of pushing back
                                    Or else
She knew I was bankrupt, a liberal has-been
In it for the memories,
She, of course, self-absorbed
Or a rebel who'd mislaid her firebrand, —
She, but a lonely thing, just dropped by,
And a dust jacket caught her eye.
It promised passion and intrigue too,
The thorny works of good and evil
As well as love of love, and not excluding
Various slaughters, the choicest sentiments.

GARDENS OF THE INTERREGNUM

1

Then I, gravitating, came to a place,
Of a parliamentary kind, innocuous.
Mackinawed authors. Rosehip tea. Leninists awash in whisky.
And for meals, hamburger-in-a-nest
Was the *Aristocratic* offering,
Broadway and Granville, Vancouver, B.C.,
Vinegar, not Nixon, up one's nose,
Let It Bleed and Altamont, northern Cal.
A darling, that girl, and I sighed a lot,
As I heard her out at her window seat,
She talking scumbags and their fashion sense:
Iron-ons and turtlenecks.

2

Oh Mary Jane and her sardonic socks,
Mary Jane and her Craven A's,
The fun she made of Diefenbaker
And the poets in serapes.
She was a Rosedale prodigy
Off-loaded on the provinces.
If the birds and the bees would soon come to die
In ways not subject to natural law,
Vermin in polluted carcasses,
Nirvana in glassy-eyed eyes,
What amused a junior-college girl,
Besides the garlic crab in Chinatown,
Was Ottawa: the rosé and the Munsinger
All sex and security breach.

Moreover, one could begin to speak, if one chose to spill,
Of credit scandals and leverage,
The running of pop guns to the Contras,
The left selling out to lifestyle.
One could begin to chart a course:
This fault line is a throughway
All the way to Baghdad in I-rak, —
That one gets you to Detroit.

3

Poke a stick in the pale part of the American eye,
And you'll know how the old stories mirror the empire,
The one-eyed Cyclops harassed, driven mad
By cheeky pirates, moviedom's Scacchi in the role of Penelope.
Nancy applied the stars to her true love Kid Ronnie
Whom we loved to hate. You see, there was
More than sheep cheese in the Frigidaire, —
There was a stash of cholinesterase inhibitors,
Angels chattering in the shade of cottonwoods, getting closer
The high-plains drifters on their horses.
Mary Jane in her knee-high socks,
Told all those poets lounging on her bed,
Grinning and shy, to behave, settle down.

4

Palermo, and one drank the finest booze,
Chatted up the ghost of Lampedusa, almond blossoms on the air
And mirages made of Arab fountains,
The sins of the fathers ziplocked
Inside basic units of heritage.
Or one was a lover-boy swinging by

At the wheel of the deucest coupe,
Come to couple and exchange true grit,
That and other copulatory fluids
In Anbar Province. As for the laws of gravity
Applied to petroleum, as for inciting a New World Order
To riot (bring on the night sticks, the tear gas, the drones),
It was late in the Cold War game, getting later, —
It was so late the Cold War had gone off
Like any meat left in the sun too long,
Resurrections nigh, Easter dreaded,
Picasso painting Lago red.

5

Whereas you, you thin-lipped ballerina,
You with the grace of a frantic pigeon,
You beheld the head of Orpheus, rancid thing,
Stuffed with poems and medicines.
It was polished smooth with the foam of the seven oceans,
Passing under the Pont de Québec.
"Cool," you said, "the future's ours.
Proto-fascists in Birkenstocks beware."

6

A woman said to me, and I believe she meant it,
Said she was going to eat her children
And then would write the book,
She with a liking for sailors,
The fedora the highlight on her head.
"How to best read John Donne,
His poetry undone by exegesis?"

Of course, she made no sense,
Her new verses all quickdraw,
Shoot-from-the-hip, no worries, mate,
She bidding me to light her cigarette,
Her eyes set on a ponytailed reprobate.

7

And you, sir, you abided a while
In a fine stone house with a valley view,
Heard out coyotes at night, sipped ice wine,
Heard out Herr Bach, f—ked yourself
Into a rogue state of bliss.
You put your Packard, Goddess of Speed,
In a time capsule, cursed the diocese.
Strictly east coast, you mentored
Neo-libs and postmodernists.
Hit man for the IMF, cocaine-ingesting bookkeeper,
You hectored the Treasury's minders.
Because the doom shout wears thin, you know,
Dies on the breezes it generates,
Catcalls, jeers, and yet more hisses
The unholy mess of democracy's scam.
Then I, gravitating, came to a place—

8

Love? Love's never at ease when power's around.
Love? Transient shadow on a slab of stone.
Love? Shadow affixed to a rose's heart.
Love? Your money or your sorry life.
Not that any of this is healthy, this musing,

The sun gone viral between swift cloud,
One thoroughly glissando in the way
One still aches from place to place—

9

There I was all London drape, just that I was in Berlin, Hotel Adlon
That survived the bombs but not the Soviets
And the schnapps. I reminisced, doing the rounds,
My sense of time a grandfather clock
That lacked for a pendulum,
Melted as if in an atomic scare.
It's not so much I was born an old soul,
Just that, Montreal-NDG and, guess what?
I've been the life of the party, engagé,
Alexandrines at the flick of a wrist almost,
Kisses to spare. Guerilla warfare.
The American way of getting to the dance?
Think Mary Jane and her research,
The way she fended off the lads
Camped outside the campaign office.
Sissboombah—
The starry, starry skies of Nevada.
Snowy Connecticut, Wal-Mart parking lot
Hard by the Trojan walls . . .

10

To the Blue Pavilion to stand them drinks,
Caligula entombed somewhere nearby . . .
Gin fizzes. Shirl sniffed her Campari,
She the quiet one. Because what's the point
Of one's premonitions, one's worst fears?

Even so, urges came on, a sudden yen for talk.
It was discussed: the foreign policy of Truman, Harry S.
Maddie, with her shimmering sequins, she
A kindly kind of vulturine bloom, curator
Of the world's earliest Henry Miller fragments,
Prophesied: *we'll be screwed, you wait and see.*

11

To which I remarked: "Maddie, dear, beautiful past measure,
Greedy in the rites of bed,
It's the barbarians who are superstitious.
Imperialists like us are all for science."

12

Tripping through the anemones, we went amongst
The republican ghosts,
The wild, keening goddesses of mountain, plain and coast,
Mixed love with scorn, tipped sword to tipped stylus.
Mallarmé and "Johnny B Goode" are also
The nub of my terrible nostalgia.

13

My terrible nostalgia, before and after
I, gravitating, came to a place,
Extended to Debussy at the ivories
In Winnaretta Singer's salon, —
To John Fahey's railroad trestles
As one might hear in the symphonies
He wrote to his dreadnought

And for all the Mary Janes.
Otherwise, Tacitus and the parasol of language
Guide my fall, even as I lie about and meander
Through the self that has no bottom.

14

And I smell the sea wind of Elba
Which was Boney's ignominy.
I smell the black-eyed hibiscus for no reason at all.
Drink the black Etruscan wine
And sign on the Phoenician's dotted line. . . .

15

And I turn this way and that and get a whiff
Of the clodded prairie and the smoke
Of Buffalo Bill's Lucretia Borgia.
Verbena in the bell towers, lemony fragrance,
And I see stacks of magazine clips . . .

16

And in my fall I tip my cap
To what it is that's come to pass:
America's drift to the deep right mystic.
The cold light of reason, though it mocks
The grandiose ceremonies of God and state,
Does not, willy-nilly, provide a respite
From the endless hurtling and the hate.
For that, what's needed
Is unfathomable mystery.

LYCIDAS REDUX

She talked to me of Sweet&Sour,
And as she talked, one could tell
That her memories of the poet
Dead now to the world—
Which is all a poet can expect these days:
To be dead now to the world—
Were affectionate, as fond as ever,
And he'd been a problematic child.

I admit, as I heard her out,
I lacked charity for the object
Of her affection, and I grew jealous, crabbed in spirit,
Envying the muse-child so sweetly dead
Now to the world, dead to the syllables
He'd counted, dead to the goodliest measures
Of her esteem and sympathies,
Seeing as she'd bedded the man
Without losing sight of reason.

                Even so, laurel and myrtle—
The old indications, ancient testaments
To poetic prowess—have gone the way of the Edsel car.
What man of verse will save himself
Through love of a critic's fond regards
When face time on Facebook or a police lineup,
When news-hour karaoke on PBS
Beat quicker paths to poetry's cash cow?

            Kindest of women when she wasn't
Primed for a break-out season, she thought it the thing to do—
It was her mission to molest the man
And make of a true poet a truer prophet,

However heavy the curse he'd bring on himself
For a state of grace unacknowledged
On any arts council Christmas list.
                                    Locusts is what she'd feed
His lyric gift, cactus thorn his satiric knack,
And for his narratives coriander, saffron, and beer.

In response to her attentions he knew new emotions,
Wept tears that were still the kind of tears
One could weigh and measure and squeeze
And so, irrigate where the postmodern sun
Still parches and dessicates and squeezes
Sand from sand, but
Even he knew he was too ugly
A Lancelot for her Guinevere.
                        She said to me, if not to the poet immortally lost
In the sensations she aroused in him,
That, yes, he was no Greek god, God knows,
Nothing handsome about him, scant loveliness,
Save for the verses that were his heart
Dedicated to the love of the unseeable
And to the malicious beauty of the visible world.
Linty bellybutton, the God-spot as well—
Akin to the effect of ringworm on his pate—
Were the special effects that persuaded editors,
Peers, competitors, hard-up lovers
To keep him quarantined, as it were,
Adored, yes, but at distance. . . .

                        Out there his ineffable penury, —
Out there the lesser boulevards
Of which he was a major bard . . .
And he was in want of lasting
Hatred for any person, of even the mildest spleen
For his chilliest detractors. A pity, that.

Noblesse oblige going manual,
It was her design, she had it in mind
To secure a weapon in his clutches.
Time for Sweet&Sour to show backbone,
Wage war against his tormentors,
Those who'd sell out transcendence for a profit,
                                who had that little trick
Of creating fire, like so: you rub items of currency together, —
You go and torch his world, —you piss on him
And then deliver, pro forma, the eulogy
To the packed hall, another one down.
You tell the lie that always raises
The roof with clamorous applause:
How poetry, in his simple thoughts,
Came to the rescue once again.

PROPERTIUS IN SNEAKERS

Kenwood trucks with gleaming stacks
Pulled flotillas of cherubs along,
Each barge on wheels a wedding cake, worlds unto themselves.
Sequined girls tossed batons, —glee-clubbers in chaps preened
    moustaches.
It was something I ate or they'd opened up—
Those minders at the gate with headphones—
A portal to places dream-strange, quantum mechanics the Bearded
    Lady.

I was waved through, —was suffused in star light.
Stations of the Cross and other sights
Greeted me in Andromeda, the chattering of starlings infinity-bound,
Language beyond the pale in Winnemucca.

So much sweet-nothing, nothing more,
Fit only for valentines and the morgue—
Love's eternity a tourist trap.
And while a gypsy read my palm,
The undersized urchin in the over-sized suit,
Contempt in his look, x-rayed the contents of my wallet.
What now to worship? Whom to adore?
I might as well have pitched my woo
At the spider on the floor.

o

Propertius in sneakers, John Donne in hip waders,
Robert Lowell in white buck dancing shoes?
Who knows what manner of man I was, Orphan Annie
The hallowed muse, in my ear conspiracy: "Pssst, Harry Potter's dead."

I was a scholar, the accent tweedy.
The Janiculum serviced my reveries

There where fauns cavorted, where a many-breasted goddess owned
March with sex rites, jasmines and bougainvillea following upon
The Saturnalia.

I was a plywood temple.
I pursued my genius.
I was incidental to the imperial design
But it needed me every now and then.

AMERICAN MOON

Grace the con, the *assurance* that things
Are under control, as when the pursuit and maintenance of power
Is the only reason to live, —
As if history cares, as if God stirs, —
As if the cherry tree in full, white-flaming blossom
But a few feet from my twilit visage
Wears a bridal dress, so I sit
On the balcony looking out at things.
And in good order night follows day,
Whatever else is in the works, —
And there's more to the moon's nether side
Than lynch mobs and decimations,
More than a turbulence of TVs, —
More than a memory of the Hochelaga—
Fish drying on their racks, the corn, —
More than the malcontents who crossed the ocean
With a hunger for Saguenay rubies . . .
Even so, could be I'm wrong, the moon all of the above and even
      more yet,
And nature's most treacherous organ squats
In the human skull, the mind formed there
And what the mind envisions
Of the sins it can bear or not. . . .
Broken cloud sky in spring, a few stars
And swatches of moonlight . . .
Arid tears and a conscience
Sometimes hard and sometimes soft
That can neither assuage a bride
Nor make things right . . .

ROME POEMS

Arrival

Went in the rain through the streets of Rome
                    according to no plan.
Came by way of the Veneto to a garden park of pine.
Knew illicit favours, the whispered coos
Of conspiracy and sex. Then air more ancient: Orpheus.
The squall passed. The sun shone, lemons bright on the trees.
And you hailed the god who brushed your lips,
And he hailed you, his snub this:
"You unconsecrated piece of work, this territory's mine.
Yours? Ohio. Which is in Cleveland."

Sculpture

Women notice, eye you, approve,
You stone satyr sprung to life.
Clusters of grapes hang from your ears,
The scent of jasmine heavy in the air.
Careful though or you'll soon be stuck
With horns more ample than the knobs
You presently sport. Yes, what paint thinner could strip away
That happy grimace from your mouth?
And who'll believe it's not always sex
That drives the engines of remonstrance,
Your heart all Roman superstition,
All the new gulags
And dead Christian grace?

From the Pages of the International Herald Tribune

So rapacious you'd even dismantle
The scaffolding's intimacy with its church.
Sacker of Rome, you not only ravish with your eyes
Cupolas and architraves, thugs of alabaster,
Things of Caravaggio and Bernini and fountains dolphin-busy,
You harvest American gazettes
For tax fraud, sex scandal and homicide
    here on a market day
    in the Campo de' Fiori.

Innocent Abroad

Through a grove of ilexes you traipsed
As though in search of a debauch.
The little white dog scampered ahead,
Sniffing every twig and rock and knapsack.
Did you expect to meet with moaning nymphs
And drunken satyrs in a shade?
Goblet in hand, Caesar's daughter
Debunking the verses of the day?
Would you get *gemütlich*, looking on,
And Watteau paint the scene?

The news all bomb blast, the dog kept romping
About with wagging tail. Mothers whispered to their infants
And boys kicked soccer balls.
Soccer balls boomed
Deep into the afternoon.
Birds piping in the pines.
Every sweet illusion true.

But something as deadly as a smile
Still danced just beyond your reach.
It drew you through light and shadow
In the balm of a warm wind.
And everything might perish and the laughter
Last forever, for as long as time was reckoned
By a marble stare. The jolly mutt, white bit of fluff,
Pricking up his ears, ready for any mystery,
To the core Roman, knew what you meant.

Invasion Force

The perfumed air was unexpected,
Time above and below you deep.
The chalk-green pool of the virgins held
The sky, would mirror roses soon.
Here amidst the forum's ruins,
American infinitude might cede
Pride of place—No such luck.

For sleek Pentecostals, armies of them,
Filed past the markets and the gods.
Unpacked cameras, heard out the guides.
The Idaho girls compared tattoos
With Connecticut counterparts,
California's best and brightest
Cold to all hegemonies but their own.

Dread is not fear so much as it's conviction
That the worst lies ahead of us, still,
The Palatine steaming from the rain,
Washington deadpan with its spin.

Roman Chanteuse

She sang as though music could die in a moment,
As though her angry eyes might not save the day.
Perhaps some letter had mentioned love
And perhaps the return letter had no answer.
Perhaps no love or song
Redeems a world ill-made.
Things happen in this cotillion
We're pleased to call time and space—

That earth and moon dance together.
That—put to fire—letters curl, flake, disintegrate.
But must narrative pursue a paradox
While all the days melt around you,
And a woman's jeering lips
Assail the pointlessness of heaven
That shimmers with its laws?

Her eyes hostages within black circles,
The entreaties in them nervous flames,
No rock-and-roll diva but a chanteuse,
She knew her songs would fade away
And the news of her death, hanging around,
Would overstay its welcome.

If you, traveller, should come across
A shiny new tomb in this town somewhere,
One tasteless in the extreme,
Have a look. It might be hers.

Urban Paradise

The rain came down in sheets.
Swallows swooped and climbed.

They scissored through the torrent
Like creatures immune to time.
A woman with garden shears
Madly snipped at garden flowers.
Madly, tulips fell.

And workmen's hammers pounded.
Drill bits chewed through stone.
Was the rain ever going to end?
     Was there such a thing as silent Rome?
A boy once said to a lonely girl,
His words at least half sincere,
"The world never changes: it's what it is,
You the sweetness at the core."

Well, perhaps the rain would end
And workmen lay their hammers down
And silence come and stay awhile
And a woman put away her giddy state
And reinstate the fallen tulips.
And I, slightly wiser or somewhat more gifted
Than a boy without an ounce of wit,
Might catch a break in this world
Of women punishing it.

Of Things to Come

What brings them, the memories that come in whispers,
Like waves that swallow waves?
Even as they diminish a man,
A man grows larger, still,
More enormous than imperial consequence,
More huge than his catastrophic loves.

A man stands at the base of three tall columns,
Saturn's old temple where once a year
Gamblers played at dice and for a day
Were one another's equals.

A man looks up, and the swirling sky
Is ominous with a Golden Age,
And vertigo, perhaps, pressurizes him,
His eyes now those of a marbled avenger.

The Year of the Four Emperors, indeed.
Was Rome mad only at the top?
What adventures in the palaces.
In the streets what mayhem.

Virgil's Exit Strategy

Even Rome couldn't duck its coming:
The boom-child and what attends it.
By all means, escape and picnic,
Sit yourself down by the willow,
The sun spreading pools on the river's surface,
A woman squatting with tissue paper
Behind a bush on the opposite bank.

As the cormorants dive and surface
And dive again and reappear to applause
And the wine rushes to your head,
Allow yourself this idle reflection:
If faith is all we get of God,
A man pitching his voice at the sun-obscured stars
Is in excess of a private creed.

Well, the eyes of the dog come to sniff you over
Are surely eternal, as eternal as the town is,

Rome still half in love with Nero,
You yourself now almost mellow,
The whole wide world a single flame
In the whirlwind of relentless change,
Time unfolding as it always has.

Romans

Romans have at one time or another made
Farce out of what's theirs alone.
What to do when it's old hat, no room left
For yet another unscheduled epiphany?
When it wears thin—the scarecrow whore,
The Pantheon dark in a thundery squall?
Announce you're moving to Yellowknife,
Cristiano will beg you to bring him along.

Still, time to step out and see what boots it—
The big, fat roses, lush air, corruptions,
The toothless waiter, chain-smoking commie,
The scaffolded villas, preening ducks,
The lacy hosiery, lazy fountains.
Sit in the breeze on the Pincio and happily
Give up numbering
All the bloated appeals for the decencies.
They'll be yours when you get home.

Barbarian at Large

A world glib and graceless?
It's as much to your liking as it is to ours.
We thank you for your honesty.
Gut-busting burgers, greasy fries,

Women whose idea of love—
A poke, a beer, and a TV flick—
All this you had, and you didn't cringe.

So what's this, you hanging around,
Walking through the groves of pine?
Well then, you're resolute. Alright, you're merely stubborn.
And then to say you love the place—
Oh dear, ill-advised. Shush or you'll annoy
The soul of it all and it fly away.

Even so, you serve notice,
If only to hear committed speech,
If only to know you've got your wits in hand,
That you're taking things for what they are,
Nothing more, nothing less:

A villa's simple absolutes,
A torso lighter than it was
Missing limbs and head.

A Moment in the Sun

Deep gold light suffuses things
And your member stirs.
A Roman sun warms your neck,
There on the Pincio, and you reflect:
Sure, the old religion went over the top
And had to die of its ungodly weight,
And science rules even as we speak,
But not now, not just yet.

Another Chanteuse

She sings, her eyelids heavy,
Her long black coat spread wide behind her
On the stone, and in this heat.
You've seen her somewhere perhaps
Rendered by Piero della Francesca, a painter whose peers
Thought him provincial and behind his time.
She doesn't do it for the money, you say,
She squeezing that accordion, making it ripple.
Tell us another.

And roses bloom. And there's a sun in the sky,
Waiters bearing trays. Spoon-eyed carabinieri cradle weapons.
Trams sail by on their allotted tracks,
Suburban Romans in spiritual transition.

The Eternal City spits and roars and mocks
As the woman sings and plays,
Offering up her chestnuts—

Oh there's room. There's room in the chatter,
                    in the cacophony of rude horns.
There's room for every suicidal mission, room for her agonies
          and those of every simpleton, and you're one of them.

And when you shove deep and reach for the coin,
And it's as though, all this while, you've been strung along,
She puts out her hand with such generous aplomb,
It would seem she's doing *you* the favour—

Immense dignity.
Captivating smile.

War Cloud

Here's what you might've done with that cloud
You believed you palavered with
When it stalled over Constantine's Arch:
Directed it east by southeast roughly,
Toward the Euphrates more or less.

Said to it: "The food and drink are passable
Where old Nineveh thrived, where Baghdad now is up for grabs.
Beware, however, the internecine rivalries,
The special ops and throwers of knives
Who, more swiftly than you can shed
Your founding fathers, will convey
You to the after-life."

As it is, even where you stand now, leaning against
                              an ancient wall,
And that's ivy reaching for your neck,
Take nothing for granted, not even the clear night sky.
For courteous demeanor, snuffling nose,
Rancid shirt, crumpled bowtie,
Belated celibacy, inconstant piety
Are, taken all together, no security, no last stand against
That loveliest of moons hanging in the pines.

Postcard

As if stone could quiver and cry
And glass be the tears, —
As if black pines could call
For a convocation of birds and they—
Parrots, peacocks, tiny swallows
Immense in their synchronized, swirling masses—
In turn shill for beauty, —

As if Nero's ghost could be allowed
To haunt the alleyways
As once he, incognito, did,
He no danger to any person, —
As if one will have no reason to hate
Even as one might say of love
That it relieves the lonely now and then
Of the weight of their disappointments— :
Moon-softened Rome in early light,
And a pilgrim keeping vigil . . .

Farewell

Voices lilt across the stone.
Oleander in the air.
A bell rings out. Another rings back,
"Why fret? God is in His heaven."

A toothless beggar, fish-like, puckers.
A sparrow picks insects off a wall.
A Roman in jeans and cowboy boots
Would snap his fingers and change it all.

You're saying "Goodbye," aren't you?
Goodbye to those brown feet in their white high heels.
To the poppies up on the Palatine.
To the dome of St Peter's.
To the hibiscus and the cirrus.
To the heat of the via Antica.
To the British accent of disdain.

And to the waiter who, caring less
For the alarm in your soul and the farewell,
Took your money with open palm
And marble stare.

CIVIL WARS

I

Love of country is a memory now
Though it was nothing more than love of place:
    Thurston County, the Puget Sound,
    The Totem Grill, the hamburger steak.
Imbiow and Murphy bent the grass
In the evergreen shadows of the seaside park
    Where one could catch an eyeful of
    Mothballed battleships,
    Grey, rusted, silent graves,
    Hull numerals ghostly white.
Imbiow and Murphy rolled around
Like tigers in ferocious play.
Perhaps it was a burgeoning romance
Or hatreds building a superstructure.
Independence Day, July fourth.
Patriots, aghast, looked on.

II

    Blue sky and flags, sun-bright balloons,
    Followed the pearly sky of a lysergic dawn.
Guitars, banjos, fiddles ensued,
Some Foggy Mountain Breakdown tune.
Movie scenes of wagon trains, whips lashing hard . . .
    California, and gold-flecked river sand
    Enchanting the grizzled forty-niners . . .
It seemed the people had majesty,
Baseballs arcing through the air,
Empire, maintenance, the setting off

Of poppers, snappers, sizzling sparklers,
Imbiow and Murphy in their clinch
Drunk on wine and "Dasein"—
That business about being there.
Apocalyptic smooches? Tongues in throats?
No doubt there was in a Cold War
Another crisis in the works.

III

How else and to what end has time passed by
From Jamestown, say, made, as it was,
      Of swamp and cypress wood,
      Mosquitoes, famine, paranoia,
      To this moment that silicon underwrites,
      And now "you've got mail," and it's as if
      We breathe for reasons other
      Than to let gas out and let gas in?
Murphy joined with a living organism,
History, that is, which is to say
The anarchist is in his grave,
      Though he spooked the Pentagon
      If not thrice-greatest Hermes,
      As he got himself discharged
      But failed to get gold from lead.
Imbiow, black-eyed Brooklynite,
Gypsy poetess,
      Still drives, so I like to think,
      A pale-green Merc, Plato and six-pack in the trunk.
She'll have seen it all: the sack of Thebes,
Rome's humiliation, Aleppo's ruin,
Shakespeare knocked off his perch,
      Thomas Jefferson not as pretty
      As once he was to young thespians.

Be it resolved that the atom bomb
Brought Japan to its knees. . . .

Even so, time was, and time remains
Skirmishes galore, epic campaigns,
Our nature changeless: generous, kind, sadistic,
    Lethal, cheap, tedious. Hedge against heaven, it's our excuse
    To crack our jokes and reap the whirlwind,
    To revere sweet clover and bird flight,
    Saturday night smack-downs and Total Divas
    And Buster Keaton on a flickering screen.

It's the fevers of mind, the revised intent
In search of lost magical purity.
It's the rhetoric of change that will attend
Each eleventh-hour closing-in on zero.
Saigon was lost and shock and awe
Broke over Baghdad between the rivers
Like a bursting sac of peekaboo eggs,
    But before all that, the Confederate states, and they wanted
    Out, the Union juggernaut shaping up,
    Lincoln's second inaugural pending. . . .

IV

Pennsylvania Avenue was an ocean of mud
On the fourth day of March in the year '65.
The capitol dome was finally built, crowning cupola
    For the grand idea. But it was *a house divided*—the republic,
    No love lost between the parts.
Under the star-swirl of a roiling cosmos,
The varied carols I hear (Whitman's parlance),
    Put to combustion, was in arrears
    To famine, exhaustion, grinding carnage.

(And ever since, the pasteboard sheen of a house of cards
Absorbs the endless seepage of the blood spilled....)
And it's all been said in a thousand books,
How it was that Lincoln took a bullet,
    Lee having thrown in the towel
    At the Appomattox Courthouse.
    Just that these bits float through me like
So much star scatter, so much Dr Pepper fizz,
So much grade-school primer dust,
So many free-floating recollections,

As when Imbiow enlisted me in her campaign,
Sticky storm night, Olympia.
Earlier in the evening, she'd removed my shirt
And unbuttoned hers, women in the room unhinged,
Men meditative, Gershwin and Jefferson Airplane
Our intermezzi, lightning tremoring in the window, —
    And then to bed, the boy in me on shaky ground,
    Imbiow pleading her fear of thunder,
    And would I hold her, or so I recall, —

And, as I do my remembering, sound waves span
Out from a church bell, holiday in progress, Quebec tropical
This far north of the compromise
That was slavers and Free Soilers, —
    This far from Atlanta burning
    As preceded Lincoln's second go-round,
    The speech he'd give pearling around
    A nicety: with malice toward none ...
    This far from Imbiow's husky laughter....

V

Years have flitted away like butterflies
Through a shadow-black forest, memory a rickety bridge

Spanning a ravine. No solid footing and yet, who knows
What might beckon to a memory in the sky?
Murphy the court jester? Imbiow the flirt?
Or Gar Cox the librarian, South Carolinian, sophisticate?
He who ate Ritalin on the job as he ransacked the books
For the dope on drugs, treated me to daiquiri-rich lunches.
    He drawled: "Gender wars, boy? Love spoiled by the letdown that
      comes
    Of shabby, unloving lust—that's what leads to lawyers."

VI

Then one is seventy, and the fool resumes
Where the fool left off, that is, with a fool's belief
    That a poem will do more than art,
    One's belief in art egregious,
    One's brain a child's brain still,
    Falling shy of mature comprehension
    Of the whys and wherefores, Christian fascists on your right,
Social justice warriors getting more incensed
As they tell you that human nature, that thing in your head,
Is a treatable disease. Havana ripe for the taking now, Castro is gone,
Artificial sweeteners stuffed in every kiss . . .

And like a man with wares to hawk
Commandeering the auction block,
The spoils of war everyone's gain
While the attack dogs are unleashed
    To secure the next arms program, it's in me even now to flog
    The goods, humanism's relics, measured lines
    With which to accompany time's mule trains
    Packing stores of drift and hell.

Unless, of course, it's finished, at last, the poetry game,
Music and thought one and the same,

The hilarity of "Euripides, Eumenides" and
Evil events from evil causes spring.
Or it's the beginning again on a return flight,
Idyll freighted here with the ancient world—
    That tree in the yard out back
    Heavy with its gleaming cherries.
    It's an Arcady item of which poets once sang
    And sing no longer, not since
    The glory days of the Marshall Plan,
    Fords on the Kurfürstendamm.
Buckley and Vidal spatting on ABC,
Priest and scientist locked in their quarrels,
Squirrels gnawing cherries as they rush
From branch to branch, starlings in on the feast,
Sparrows in steep-banked flight, robins lilting
On the ground, all speak to this: at stake how tell a tale of living,
    How interpret the stars, how best eat a fig
    And proceed, love undiminished.

SARASOTA BEACH

And yet, from a pretty terrace, the sun setting nicely
Down
Like an animal nestling into sleep,
With a Midwesterner's eyes you beheld the ocean
As it glittered, —saw its dancing, bird-riven sparklets,
Birds beyond number in the sweep of a glance,

And it was
A silhouette of the great world.

And it was the dying and the bliss,
You quickening to a world so far away
From Ohio, from the condo-throttled beach,
Snowbirds TV-ing in their living rooms.
Your hand held in mine a butterfly
That one cups and then releases,
Was love's tender burden:
That we kiss and are alone,
That we kiss and are at one
With one another's breathing,
It being so much—the spectacle of the bird-cloaked sea
In our humbled sight, —it being nothing at all—
Our view of the emerging star-lit firmament.

PASSACAGLIA

Once again for the goodness of measure,
And I have stood by the sea and looked out at it, small,
The sea-wide restlessness immense,
The waves seeming to confess—
In their rising, cresting, crashing,
In their rolling sweep across the distances—
That they could not help but be what they are
In their relentless successions, in each of those successions
A longing for the rocky or sandy shore
And the stone faces against which they pound.

Like this I have stood by the sea on two continents,
Semi-conscious, restless myself,
The mutterings of poets in my alembic shadow, —
In me wine or Southern Comfort or other brew, —
In my eyes the luminescence tide-carried late at night
In which the sparking embers of driftwood fires
Rose and fell cold, —in my eyes the sun-sparkles, the sunset glitter,
And the feeding birds ascending and swooping down
Like a single creature in their thousands.

And who in this world couldn't fail to see
That it is the lightest world of all the worlds
That came before it, the bother of truth off-loaded, consequence
    cancelled
Or neutralized (as when medicines overrun infection
And casuists on talk shows spin their talking points
Like so many Fates carrying the day
On the strength of so many megahertz), the dancing sea for good or ill
A moon-bright do-si-do perpetual motion.
Its song has no end but no substance either

As in edict or monument and yet, it's as though
Humankind is now sea-like itself.

o

Again, for the goodness of measure,
And that humankind, a force among others
Like the wind and the tide and volcanic upsurges,
Is neither praise-good nor blameworthy, is and will be, and will
   glitter,
And hang around indifferent and bored,
And it will destroy, changing what it touches.
The difference is, and here's the thing:
The sea does not tire of itself and so
Commit intransigence against the spirit of life.
Humankind, oh humankind (each separate body of which
Is a packet of neurons and other determinants),
Weary of its self-infatuation, the gods defunct,
Furloughed, sent packing, superseded,
On occasion loathes itself for the lies it tells
Of its genius and transcendence.

o

Again, for the goodness of measure,
And the hearth and the bed, the shed and the shitter
Haunted by gods, by human hands made,
From these structures stem
Human arrangements such as obtain now,
Come to us by way of castle and palace, hut and stockade,
Come upon the glass tower and the airport lounge
Where one holds up to the light of the sun
A martini and the state of one's luck.
For instance, can you see her—the goddess Isis,
Lunar crown on her head, sistrum rattling
Like the rattle-end of a venomous snake
                                    though she's beneficent, —

She, in her mother's womb, joined with Osiris her brother—
                'perfect sexual union,' concord of sorts?
And can you hear the hoot, the toot, the whistle, the puffing steam
Of the calliope at carnival near her temple couch,
And all the rhyming seasons and all the good prayer alongside the
    great river
That was love of bird and beast and humankind
In the revolutions of the moon? And so, it went:
Black bread, black beer, black god, the polished diorite stone
For centuries and thousands of years, and then later—tourists,
Napoleonic in their enthusiasms, Isis a catalogued memory,
Scuttling up and down the pyramids . . .

o

And the good measure once familiar to us
Is shattered, blasted by a scream, if not by the corrosive hum
Of microprocessors that—
In their aggregate—are search and destroy.
No matter that the goodness we knew
Was an illusion, mirage born of the sun risen on folly,
But that Greeks saw the origins of sin
In hubris and blind spots, all of it grating on the soul,
So much so that it always flees the room
Even as one laughs at the joke just relayed, —
Or that Dante saw in God the soul's timorous quest,
Or that Zola made of justice humankind's prime jurisprudence,
As have countless novelists in smoking jackets, —no matter that the
    Romans,
Perhaps the cruelest of imperial masters, even so, saw in the jilting of
    Dido
That Aeneas would settle unease forever on the Roman mind.

o

Once again for the goodness of measure,
And from Thamesport to Antwerp to the Gulf of St Lawrence

And inwards to Montreal past Quebec
And the tight bend in the river there
(Tight for a ship 400 metres in length),
I need not have troubled myself with words like *Thalassa*,
Sailing, as we did, along a marine boulevard
In a world of hyper-markets, but even so
I sustained a kind of wonder from that sail on the ocean, and the
      wonder was
The earth itself, the horizon limned with sun,
The sun-touched curvature which rendered me small,
And this in view of the laws which we outgrow, the outstripping
Leaving us between faiths and knowing it all.
So then, by code or unwritten scruples, here and there
In pockets, enclaves, *arrondissements* of the psyche peopled by
      believers
And skeptics, by bits and pieces of humankind
Cursed with good will, some live to keep intact
The miracle of wonder,
                            for instance, that bowl of sky beneath which the
      ship went its way
Keeping off thunder, its colour robin's-egg blue and cerise.
And there is relation between the bridge of one's nose and the arcing
      dolphin,
Between the sin of Cain and the sin of Agamemnon
And the sin of Clytemnestra, flaming ice in her veins,
Nausea in her gut, her eyes distillates of vengeance,
And the building wave that must swell and crest and fall
And die on a sandy or rocky shore, its measuring sweep
Collapsed
Until the next incursion and foaming and settling among
Pebbles and shell-bits and sand-grains, and then the next measure.

TO MARY

I am, my sweet, the fattest thin man
On our fair stretch of boulevard.
 I eat my greens, I drink my wine and curse
 The Executive and worse.

Early Autumn, more hot days to come,
And I follow the lives of birds.
 Surely, they suffer in this heat.
 Surely, they pay taxes to Parliament.
 Surely, they're comedians.

Will you trifle with me and then give
No less than evil the slip,
 Have me come love you in a realm
 Where birds fly more freely, because more pristine?
 From what could I ever have saved you?

I am, my sweet, the fattest thin man
On our stretch of fair boulevard.
 I eat my greens, I drink my wine, and I believe
 Everything and nothing, —I believe in you

Even as you accept what I assume
Is the cause in some of hysterics, in others of mirth:
 We're interlopers on this earth.

Acknowledgments are due to Marc Plourde, Michael Glover, Amanda Jernigan, MH, *Nikas*, and two Armenians.

Earlier versions of a few of these poems appeared in *The Bow-Wow Shop* and *Canadian Notes & Queries*.

Born in Oberammergau in 1947, Norm Sibum grew up in Germany, Alaska, Missouri, Utah, and Washington. He has been a Montrealer since 1994. Along with Bruce Serafin, he founded the *Vancouver Review* in 1989 and he has published several collections of poetry in Canada and in England with Carcanet Press. His *Girls and Handsome Dogs* (Porcupine's Quill, 2002) won the Quebec Writer's Federation A.M. Klein Award for Poetry. *The Pangborn Defence* (Biblioasis, 2008) was shortlisted for the same award.